ED

# Clara Barton

### History Maker Bios

## Candice Ransom

LERNER PUBLICATIONS COMPANY • MINNEAPOLIS

*To the always energetic Su*

Illustrations by Tim Parlin

Text copyright © 2003 by Candice Ransom
Illustrations copyright © 2003 by Lerner Publications Company

Lerner Publications Company
A division of Lerner Publishing Group
241 First Avenue North
Minneapolis, MN 55401 U.S.A.

Website address: www.lernerbooks.com


Library of Congress Cataloging-in-Publication-Data

Ransom, Candice F., 1952–
    Clara Barton / by Candice Ransom.
        p.    cm. — (History maker bios)
    Includes bibliographical references and index.
    ISBN: 0–8225–4677–9 (lib. bdg. : alk. paper)
    1. Barton, Clara, 1821–1912—Juvenile literature. 2. Red Cross—United States—Biography—Juvenile literature. 3. Nurses—United States—Biography—Juvenile literature. [1. Barton, Clara, 1821–1912. 2. Nurses. 3. Women—Biography.] I. Title. II. Series.
    HV569.B3 R35 2003
    361.7'634'092—dc21                                                    2002006470

Manufactured in the United States of America
1  2  3  4  5  6  –  JR  –  08  07  06  05  04  03

# TABLE OF CONTENTS

# INTRODUCTION

Clara Barton spent her whole life helping people. During the Civil War, she risked her own safety to bring food and medical help to soldiers. Later she started the American Red Cross, a group that gives aid to victims of disasters and wars.

For many years, Clara seemed too timid to do such important things. As a child, she was terrified by thunderstorms, snakes, and strangers. When she became a teacher, she was afraid to stand up in front of her class.

But whenever she saw people in trouble, Clara forgot her fears. She braved bullets to nurse wounded soldiers. She helped people caught in floods and forest fires.

Many people have called Clara Barton a hero. Clara believed her job was to be brave for others.

This is her story.

# 1 SHY LITTLE GIRL

**O**n Christmas Day in 1821, a little girl was born in North Oxford, Massachusetts. The baby was named Clarissa Harlowe Barton, but she was nicknamed Clara.

Like many New England children, Clara started school at an early age. She was just three when she surprised her teacher by spelling "artichoke" on the first day of school. She already knew how to read, too.

Clara loved learning about the stars and ancient Rome. But the other children at school made her feel shy. Her family found that she learned best at home on their farm with the help of her brothers and sisters. Sally taught her poetry. Stephen was her math teacher. David gave her horseback riding lessons.

*Clara was born in this house in North Oxford, Massachusetts. Her older brothers and sisters called her Tot because she was many years younger than they were.*

*David Barton was Clara's favorite brother.*

Clara grew up timid. She ran away from snakes and hid from thunderstorms. But when her brothers were around, she turned into a bold tomboy. She tossed balls and climbed trees. She loved to listen to her father talk about his days as a soldier, too.

When Clara was eleven, David fell from a barn roof. He wasn't hurt badly, but his headache and fever wouldn't go away. Clara became his nurse. For two years, she gave him his medicine and fed him.

Slowly, David got better. Clara was glad, but she missed being a nurse. She liked having someone need her.

As a teenager, Clara was still shy, and her feelings were easily hurt. Once she rushed to her room in tears because her mother wanted her to wear shabby gloves. Her parents worried about her.

A family friend suggested that Clara needed some sort of meaningful work. Maybe she should become a teacher. The thought of being alone with a roomful of children frightened Clara. But she decided to try.

## HELPING THOSE IN NEED

Clara spent much of her free time working with poor families in North Oxford. She helped children with their schoolwork. She asked her father to give money to the hungry. She took care of the sick, too. Once she even caught smallpox from a family she was nursing. She was lucky to survive the disease.

On her first day as a teacher, eighteen-year-old Clara had no idea what to do with her class. So she read from the Bible. To her surprise, all forty students listened. When some boys became rowdy at recess, Clara joined their ball game. They were impressed by her skill at throwing. Maybe being a teacher wasn't so hard after all.

For the next ten years, Clara taught in different schools around North Oxford. Her friends got married and had children. But that life wasn't for Clara. She wanted to be treated as an equal. Most men wouldn't treat her that way.

Clara at age twenty-nine. This photograph was taken at the Clinton Liberal Institute, where Clara spent half a year studying.

*Clara's school drew in so many eager students that Clara gave up her own chair to make space for one more.*

In 1852, Clara moved to Bordentown, New Jersey. She noticed boys hanging around in the streets. In many places, people had to pay to send their children to school. These boys were too poor to pay. So Clara started a free school.

Clara's school grew to six hundred students. The townspeople built a bigger school. But they hired a man to run it. They didn't think a woman could do the job.

Clara was so upset that she became ill. She decided to move somewhere warmer to improve her health. In 1854, she boarded a train for a new life in Washington, D.C.

# 2 CIVIL WAR NURSE

Clara got a job as a clerk for the United States government. She felt lucky— very few women could get a job like hers. For a few years, she copied papers by hand in her neat writing.

In the city's newspapers, Clara read about trouble in the nation. The North and the South had disagreed about slavery for a long time. Black people were kept as slaves in Southern states. Northern states wanted to make slavery against the law.

In 1860, Abraham Lincoln was elected president. He had often spoken against slavery. After his election, the Southern states broke away from the United States. They formed the Confederate States of America. In April 1861, the Civil War began.

*Many people supported the election of Abraham Lincoln. But others were angry. For his own safety, the new president arrived in Washington, D.C., in disguise.*

*Civil War soldiers faced terrible danger for low pay. This man fought for the Union.*

President Lincoln called for volunteers to defend the Union. Soldiers headed for Washington, D.C., to answer the call. Remembering her father's war stories, Clara longed to be a soldier, too. But women were not allowed to join the army.

Clara wondered how she could help her country. Then Massachusetts troops were attacked as they traveled to Washington. When Clara met their train, she was shocked to see some of her former students among the wounded. Boys she knew had been hurt by the war!

She felt even angrier when she learned that Washington had no army hospitals. The wounded soldiers were put in office buildings. Even worse, the army had given the men no food.

Clara bought all the food she could afford. At home, she emptied her drawers of thimbles, sewing thread, buttons, combs, and other useful items. Then she took baskets of supplies to the Massachusetts soldiers.

The men were grateful for the small comforts Clara brought. The soldiers needed her! She had found a way to help.

A soldier's sewing kit. Many of the troops Clara helped had almost no supplies.

A few weeks later, Clara heard the distant boom of cannons. On July 21, Confederate forces defeated the Union army at Bull Run in Virginia. Soon Washington was filled with the wounded.

Nurses led by Dorothea Dix tended to the men. Clara could have asked to join them, but Miss Dix was stern. Clara didn't want to work for her. She would do the most good working on her own.

## MISS DIX'S RULES

Dorothea Dix worried that her nurses would flirt with soldiers. She would allow only women over thirty to become nurses. They had to be plain and could wear only brown or black. Clara was over thirty, but she was *not* plain. She liked pretty green dresses. She wore makeup, too. Dorothea Dix wouldn't have approved of her at all!

Clara took supplies to the soldiers, as she had done before. But she realized that they needed more than jellies and combs. Many men were dying on the battlefields, before they could be brought to Washington. The Union army didn't have enough bandages, medicine, or nurses to save them.

Clara went into action. She asked friends for help. They sent enough supplies to fill three warehouses.

*These Illinois women gathered food and made clothes to send to Union soldiers.*

*Some women took part in the war by following husbands who joined the army. Such women cooked and washed clothes for soldiers in camp.*

Next Clara needed to get the army's permission to take her supplies to the battlefields. She felt shy and afraid. The army wouldn't want a woman in the middle of a men's war.

But she had to ask. Wearing a plain dress so that she would look serious, she went to see Colonel Daniel Rucker at the War Department.

Sure enough, Rucker told her that women didn't belong on battlefields. Clara swallowed hard and said that she wasn't scared. Then she described her three warehouses full of supplies. Impressed, Rucker gave her permission to go.

In August 1862, the armies clashed in Virginia. Clara and two helpers loaded supplies into a railroad car and rushed to the scene. What she saw made her shudder with horror. Men lay on the ground, covered with blood and moaning in pain. Some had lost arms or legs in the fighting.

Clara was shocked by the suffering. But she wasn't afraid to help the wounded men through their agony. For two days and nights she nursed them in houses, churches, and barns.

Clara during the Civil War

By the time Clara's supplies were gone, she was bone tired. But she knew her work had saved many lives. She headed home for a short rest.

Two weeks later, she heard cannons again from Bull Run. Hurrying to help, she found thousands of wounded men lying in the dirt or on beds of hay. Clara bandaged wounds and made slings for broken arms. She fed the men soup made from wine, cracker crumbs, and sugar. "You must not give up," she told them in a firm, gentle voice.

At the age of forty, Clara Barton had found a new life as a Civil War nurse.

# 3 ANGEL OF THE BATTLEFIELD

**A**fter a few days of rest, Clara and her wagon of supplies were on the move again. She followed Union troops to Antietam, Maryland. Once more the armies were fighting.

For the first time, Clara found herself nursing right on the edge of a battle. With shells bursting around her, she dashed from one wounded man to another. As she gave a soldier some water, a bullet tore through her sleeve and struck him in the chest. He was killed. Clara never mended her sleeve.

Minutes later, she used her own penknife to perform her first operation. A soldier was in agony from a bullet lodged in his cheek. All the surgeons were too busy to bother with such a small wound. Clara gritted her teeth and removed the bullet.

The Battle of Antietam was the bloodiest day of the Civil War. About 7,700 troops died, and many more were wounded.

## LIGHTS IN THE DARKNESS

As night fell during the Battle of Antietam, Clara found the commanding doctor in despair. He had no lamps, and he couldn't work in the dark. He expected five hundred men to die that night. Then Clara showed him the dozens of lanterns she had brought. Their light let the work of saving soldiers continue through the night.

The firing grew so fierce that it scared off all the male army nurses from the farmhouse where Clara was working. All the doctors left except one. Clara was frightened, too, but she wasn't about to leave the wounded troops who needed her. She stayed and helped the remaining doctor perform an operation.

After the battle, a doctor named James Dunn called Clara "the angel of the battlefield." While men killed each other, she spread kindness and comfort.

*The Battle of Fredericksburg was a terrible defeat for the Union army.*

The war went on and on. That December, the armies fought in Fredericksburg, Virginia. Clara set up a hospital in a large house. By now, the Union army depended on her.

More than 12,600 Union men were wounded or killed in the battle. The wounded filled every room of the house. Some were even stacked on cupboard shelves.

For more than two weeks, Clara bathed wounds, washed faces, wrote letters for those unable to write, and said prayers for the dying. At night, she slept in a tent beside her wagon.

Clara returned to Washington on the last day of 1862. She had become famous for her deeds at Antietam and Fredericksburg. Officers saluted her on the streets. Soldiers she had nursed visited her. Senators held a party in her honor.

In 1863, she collected more supplies, then nursed soldiers in South Carolina. But by 1864, Dorothea Dix's nurses were working in battlefield hospitals. The army Clara had once supplied had plenty of food, blankets, medicine, and clothing. How could she help now?

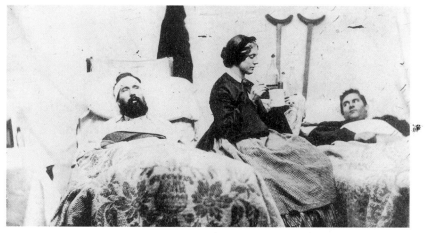

*Many women besides Clara did all they could to help soldiers on both sides of the war. This nurse stirs a drink for wounded men in Nashville, Tennessee.*

Then Clara learned of two fierce battles in Virginia. The fighting was much worse than anyone had expected. Clara was needed—quickly. She hurried aboard a steamboat, taking only coffee and two kettles.

Heavy spring rains were falling when she landed near Fredericksburg, where the wounded had been sent. Almost four hundred wagons loaded with men were stuck in mud. Clara boiled coffee and fed the starving men crackers that another volunteer had brought.

General Ulysses S. Grant led the Union army during the last year of the war. Later he became president of the United States.

The next day, she made her way into town. Churches, warehouses, and even stables had been turned into hospitals.

Clara tended to the men without resting. Though she was often tired, she did her best to show her patients a cheerful face. One of those she helped was her own cousin, Ned Barton.

Next Clara went to Petersburg, another Virginia city. The heat was unbearable. The armies fought around the city all summer and into the fall. Clara treated men for sunburn, mosquito bites, and heatstroke. She organized nurses and set up hospitals.

Her work was coming to an end. On April 9, 1865, the top Confederate general, Robert E. Lee, surrendered to the Union's Ulysses S. Grant. The long war was finally over.

# 4 AFTER THE WAR

The war had changed the nation in many ways. President Lincoln died on April 15, 1865, shot by a Confederate supporter named John Wilkes Booth. Congress was planning to ban slavery forever. And hundreds of thousands of men on both sides had been killed or were missing.

Clara had a pile of letters about those missing men. It seemed that everyone in America knew her name. Even before the war ended, she had begun to receive mail from the worried relatives of soldiers. Had she cared for their loved ones? Did she know what had happened to them?

It wasn't easy to write down names during a battle. Clara had made notes about the men she cared for, but most hospitals had no records at all. Still, she figured out a way to find some of the missing men.

*Thousands of people filled the streets to share their grief during the funeral procession of President Lincoln.*

Clara sent lists of the missing to newspapers. People wrote to her about soldiers they had nursed in their homes.

The most information came from a remarkable young man named Dorence Atwater. He was a Union soldier who had been held prisoner in Andersonville, Georgia. Thousands of Union men starved to death or died of disease at Andersonville. They were buried in graves marked with numbered sticks, but no names.

## CIVIL WAR PRISONS

Thousands of soldiers died in prison camps on both sides of the Civil War. Both the North and the South took more prisoners than their prisons could safely hold. Neither side had enough supplies to feed and clothe the men. The soldiers' suffering has not been forgotten. The prison at Andersonville is now a national park. It honors all Americans who have been held prisoner during any war.

*Thanks to Clara's work, stones mark each grave at Andersonville with the name and the home state of the soldier buried there.*

Confederate officers had made Atwater work as a clerk in the prison. His job was to keep a list of the men who died and their grave numbers. Atwater wrote a second, secret copy of his list. When he was freed, he smuggled this copy back to the North.

In July 1865, Clara and Atwater went to Andersonville. Thanks to Atwater's list, 13,000 graves were marked with the names of the brave men who lay there. Clara helped make sure that the names of the dead were made public, too.

It was expensive to track down missing soldiers. Clara needed money. She decided to tour the country as a speaker.

People were happy to pay to hear Clara tell about her life as a battlefield nurse. Former soldiers greeted her after her speeches, thanking her for nursing them. People handed her flowers. Many told her they had named daughters after her.

Though Clara loved the attention, she did not enjoy speaking in public. Standing in front of large groups terrified her. During a speech in Maine in 1868, Clara lost her voice. She hadn't rested since the beginning of the war. Now she was tired and ill.

In four years, Clara had learned the fate of more than 22,000 missing men. She was glad she could help, but it was time for another change. In August 1869, she boarded a ship for Europe.

# 5 THE RED CROSS

**C**lara settled in Geneva, Switzerland, hoping the crisp air would restore her health. There she met a doctor named Louis Appia. He told her about a group called the Red Cross.

This organization had been formed to help soldiers in battle. Wherever fighting took place, Red Cross volunteers cared for the wounded on both sides. These workers were protected from harm. They wore a badge with a red cross to show they belonged to the organization.

Thirty-two nations had joined the Red Cross when Clara learned about it. The United States wasn't a member—but she was sure it ought to be.

In 1870, France went to war with Germany. Clara saw a chance to become part of the Red Cross herself.

The Red Cross symbol could be understood by people all over Europe, no matter what language they spoke.

She forgot about her health problems and signed on as a volunteer. Clara worked mostly with families torn apart by the war. She gave out food, clothing, and money. And as always, she offered comfort.

In 1873, Clara sailed home. She had worked too hard and was ill again. For the next two years, Clara could not write, read, or even comb her hair. She went to a hospital in Dansville, New York. Fresh air, good food, and plenty of rest cured her.

Clara hard at work for the Red Cross in Germany

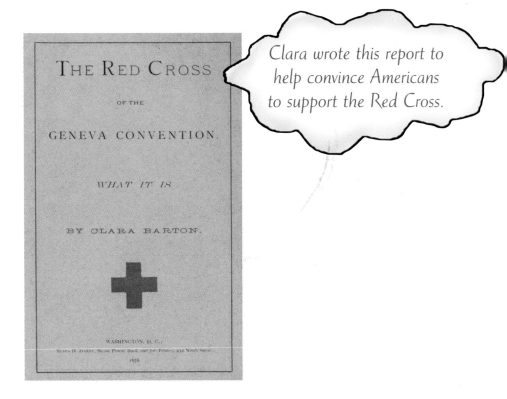

Clara hadn't forgotten the Red Cross. She decided to start an American branch. To do so, she would have to convince the United States government to sign an agreement with all the Red Cross nations. She wrote to officials in Washington and asked senators for help.

After six years of work, Clara succeeded. In 1881, the American Red Cross was formed. At age fifty-nine, she was its first president.

That fall, forest fires raged across Michigan. Though the Red Cross was created to aid soldiers during war, Clara felt it should help people during peacetime, too. She led her workers into action. They collected money, tools, clothing, and bedding for the victims of the fires.

The work was just beginning. In 1884, floods washed across Ohio and Indiana. Clara rented a steamboat to haul Red Cross supplies. After seeing Clara deliver food and rescue stranded animals, everyone knew that the red cross on the boat's flag stood for help.

## THE LITTLE SIX

In 1884, six Pennsylvania children gave the Red Cross $51.25. Clara saved the money until she met six children who lived in a barn with their mother. Clara gave this family the money raised by the "Little Six." The kindness of the Little Six moved many people to give to the Red Cross.

There were disasters nearly every year. In 1889, heavy spring rains caused a dam to burst near Johnstown, Pennsylvania. Almost three thousand people were killed by the flood that resulted. Most of the city was left underwater.

Clara braved the floodwaters to travel to the scene. Using a packing crate as a desk, she wrote letters asking for supplies and volunteers. Lumber, clothing, and food were shipped to the area. Three shelters were built for the homeless.

Flooding in 1889 destroyed many homes in Johnstown, Pennsylvania. Almost every family in the city lost at least one member.

*Swirling winds and flooding rains make hurricanes the most deadly kind of storm. This hurricane was photographed from outer space.*

Five months later, Clara left Johnstown. The newspaper expressed the city's thanks to her. "Try to describe the sunshine, try to describe the starlight. Words fail."

Clara loved her work, but it wasn't easy to go on year after year. In 1893, a hurricane hit the Sea Islands off the coast of South Carolina. Clara had few helpers, and funds were low. At age seventy-two, she was tired. But 35,000 people were homeless and starving. She couldn't ignore the call for help.

The Red Cross helped people in the Sea Islands help themselves. These farmers prepared a donation of potatoes to plant in place of a lost crop.

Clara traveled to the islands and gave out clothing and food. Most importantly, she convinced the government to send cotton seeds. With the seeds, farmers could replant crops that had washed away. They could earn a living and rebuild their lives.

The Red Cross took Clara outside the United States, too. In February 1898, she sailed to Cuba, where people were fighting for freedom from Spain. Clara wanted to help war prisoners, who needed food and care.

Weeks later, the United States joined the war against Spain. Now Clara worked sixteen hours a day in battlefield hospitals. It was terrible to see men being wounded and killed again. But this time, at least the Red Cross was able to help.

The United States won the war in December 1898. Back home, Clara met a new kind of trouble. The Red Cross had grown into a large organization. Some members suggested that she was too old to be president.

Clara, seated in front, in Cuba at age seventy-seven

Clara was stung by these comments. But she kept working quietly at her house in Glen Echo, Maryland, which also served as the Red Cross headquarters. Then, in 1904, she was asked to step down as president.

At first, she refused. Eighty was not too old to be a good leader! But people complained that Red Cross money wasn't being used properly. The complaints weren't true, but Clara was tired. In May, she resigned.

It was the saddest day of her life. She wondered what to do next.

*Clara and friends at her house in 1904. She stands second from the left.*

The angel of the battlefield at age eighty-four

Soon she found an answer. She helped start the National First Aid Association of America to teach people how to care for those harmed by accidents. First aid students learned to apply a bandage and splint a broken arm.

Clara also wrote books and worked in her garden at home. On April 12, 1912, she died in Glen Echo. She was ninety years old.

Friends, retired soldiers, and former students came to her funeral. They remembered a woman who devoted her life to helping others. She believed in being useful. Whenever she saw a need, Clara Barton filled it, often alone.

And she was not afraid.

# TIMELINE

CLARA BARTON WAS BORN
ON DECEMBER 25,
1821.

## In the year . . .

1833   she nursed her brother David after he fell from a barn roof.

1840   she became a teacher.   Age 18

1852   she started a free school for poor children in New Jersey.

1854   she moved to Washington, D.C.   Age 32

1861   the Civil War began.
she collected supplies for Union troops.

1862   she nursed wounded soldiers on battlefields   Age 40
in Virginia and Maryland.

1863   she helped troops in South Carolina.

1864   she returned to Virginia to nurse on battlefields there.

1865   the Civil War ended.
President Abraham Lincoln was killed.
she searched for missing soldiers.
she traveled to a Confederate prison in Andersonville, Georgia.

1869   she went to Europe and learned about the Red Cross.

1870   she became a Red Cross volunteer.

1881   she founded the American Red Cross.   Age 59

1898   she nursed American soldiers in Cuba.

1904   she was asked to step down as Red Cross   Age 82
president.

1905   she helped start the National First Aid Association of America.

1912   she died in Glen Echo, Maryland.   Age 90

# THE AMERICAN RED CROSS

During the Civil War, Clara Barton proved that a woman could work on the battlefield with courage and strength. She helped thousands of soldiers and saved many lives. Yet she may have made her biggest mark on the world by founding the American Red Cross. This organization has brought aid and comfort to people for more than 120 years.

The American Red Cross has brought medical help to soldiers in many wars and battles. Its workers have helped disaster victims cope with hurricanes, tornadoes, and fires. A blood donation program provides blood for injured people who need it to live. And Red Cross classes offer information about first aid, healthy nutrition, and ways to avoid disease. To find out more about the work of the American Red Cross and how kids can be a part of it, visit <http://www.redcross.org/services/youth/kids/>.

*Children in Somalia, Africa, receive bags of supplies from the American Red Cross.*

# Further Reading

NONFICTION

Blashfield, Jean F. *Women at the Front: Their Changing Roles in the Civil War*. Danbury, CT: Franklin Watts, 1997. Traces the work of Clara Barton and other Civil War women who nursed the wounded, provided food and clothing for the armies, or even disguised themselves as men to fight.

Gale, Karen Buhler. *The Kids' Guide to First Aid*. Charlotte, VT: Williamson Publishing, 2002. Readers who share Clara's interest in first aid will find this book a helpful introduction to how to care for others in an emergency.

Ransom, Candice. *Children of the Civil War*. Minneapolis: Carolrhoda Books, 1998. Describes the lives of children in the North, the South, and their armies during the Civil War.

FICTION

Osborne, Mary Pope. *After the Rain: Virginia's Civil War Diary, Book Two*. New York: Scholastic, 2002. A ten-year-old girl's family spends the final months of the Civil War in Washington, D.C., where President Lincoln is assassinated in April 1865.

Polacco, Patricia. *Pink and Say*. New York: Philomel, 1994. In this moving Civil War picture book, two teenage soldiers—one white, the other African American—support each other through the horror of battle and imprisonment at Andersonville.

Ransom, Candice. *The Promise Quilt*. New York: Walker & Co., 1999. When Addie loses her father during the Civil War, Mama helps her regain hope by making a quilt that only Addie can complete.

# WEBSITES

**American Red Cross Virtual Museum and History**
<http://www.redcross.org/services/youth/kids/museum.html>
Learn about the history of the Red Cross and what kids
have done to help people in need for more than 120 years.

**Clara Barton National Historic Site**
<http://www.nps.gov/clba/> Clara's final home has been
made a museum to honor her memory. Website visitors can
view photographs of Clara, read her writing about the Red
Cross, and follow a timeline of her life.

# SELECT BIBLIOGRAPHY

Barton, Clara. *A Story of the Red Cross.* 1904. Reprint, New
York: Airmont Books, 1968.

Barton, William Eleazor. *The Life of Clara Barton.* 1922.
Reprint, New York: AMS Press, 1969.

Buckingham, Clyde. *Clara Barton: A Broad Humanity.*
Alexandria, VA: Mount Vernon Publishing, 1977.

Oates, Stephen B. *A Woman of Valor: Clara Barton and the
Civil War.* New York: The Free Press, 1994.

Pryor, Elizabeth Brown. *Clara Barton: Professional Angel.*
Philadelphia: University of Pennsylvania Press, 1987.

Ross, Ishbel. *Angel of the Battlefield: The Life of Clara
Barton.* New York: Harper, 1956.

Young, Charles Sumner. *Clara Barton.* Boston: R. G.
Badger, 1922.

# INDEX

## Acknowledgments

**For photographs and artwork:** Clara Barton National Historic Site/National Park Service, pp. 4, 10, 36, 38, 41, 42, 43; Library of Congress #USZ62–093974, p. 7; Library of Congress #USZ62–113044, p. 8; © Lee Snider/CORBIS, p. 11; © Independent Picture Service, p. 13. Joel Emmons Whitney, Minnesota Historical Society, p. 14; Minnesota Historical Society, p. 15; Chicago Historical Society, ICHI-22,103, p. 17; Library of Congress #LC-B8171–2405, p. 18; Library of Congress #ZC4–6307, p. 19; Library of Congress, pp. 22, 24; © Todd Strand/Independent Picture Service, p. 23. © Leib Image Archives, p. 25; Minneapolis Public Library, p. 26; Library of Congress # LC–BH834–32, p. 29; © Raymond Gehman/CORBIS, p. 31; © Corbis Royalty Free Images, p. 34; © Bettmann/CORBIS, p. 35; National Oceanic & Atmospheric Administration, p. 39; Library of Congress # USZ262–122102, p. 40; American Red Cross, p. 45. Front cover, American Red Cross. Back cover, © Todd Strand/Independent Picture Service.
**For quoted material:** p. 20, James Dunn to his wife, quoted in undated newspaper clipping, "The Angel of the Battlefield," Clara Barton Papers, Library of Congress; p. 23, Clara Barton to "Dear Friends," September 4, 1862, Clara Barton Papers, Library of Congress; p. 39, "Farewell to Miss Barton," *Johnstown Daily Tribune,* October 23, 1889.